Deluxe Edition

Collected from the Guardiand's and
the Telegraph's "the 100 greatest novels of all time" list.

Preserved the original format whilst repairing
imperfections present in the aged copy.

See the complete list at
iboo.com

Diane Mayer Christiansen Releases Survivor: Out of the Wild, A Dystopian Novel of Struggle and Triumph

One Couple is Separated at World's End, The Fight to Reunite is Only Half the Battle

CHICAGO, ILLINOIS, UNITED STATES, January 4, 2021 /EINPresswire.com/ --

by Hannah SPRAKER

Award-Winning Author, Diane Mayer Christiansen is proud to announce the release of her latest book, Survivor: Out of the Wild. In her latest young-adult dystopian novel, Diane takes readers on a thrilling post-apocalyptic adventure after the world is destroyed by a solar flare. Following a 50-year frozen sleep to escape the destruction of the world, one couple is separated, and their mission is to stay alive and perhaps, reunite.

Simultaneously following two protagonists, Wren and Aiden, in parallel; Diane masterfully balances each perspective as the characters try to make it to the safety of the new world, built by a new government. A story of destruction, rebirth, and triumph, Survivor encompasses various themes of self-love and growth as both characters struggle with differ-ent feelings of inadequacies, fighting to overcome each obstacle that comes in each of their paths. Paralleling the external struggle with internal struggles many young adults face today, Diane Mayer Christiansen's mission to illustrate strength, love, and character in the face of adversity, bleeds off of each page while tugging on every heart-string. Set to be a must-read for young adults, Survivor is harnessing praise near and far for the brilliance in character development.

"More care is put into the charac-ters than many books of its ilk. The disconnect between the two protag-onists--one still carries a flame, one still carries regret--is compelling, and the emotional anguish of characters in a sinister and traumatizing position is realized effectively."
- Publishers Weekly Booklife Review

Through proof of concept, dedica-tion to the craft, and unwavering commitment to building a platform

SURVIVOR
OUT OF THE WILD

NE MAYER CHRISTIANSEN

Diane Mayer Christiansen's mission to illustrate strength, love, and character in the face of adversity, bleeds off of each page while tugging on every heartstring.

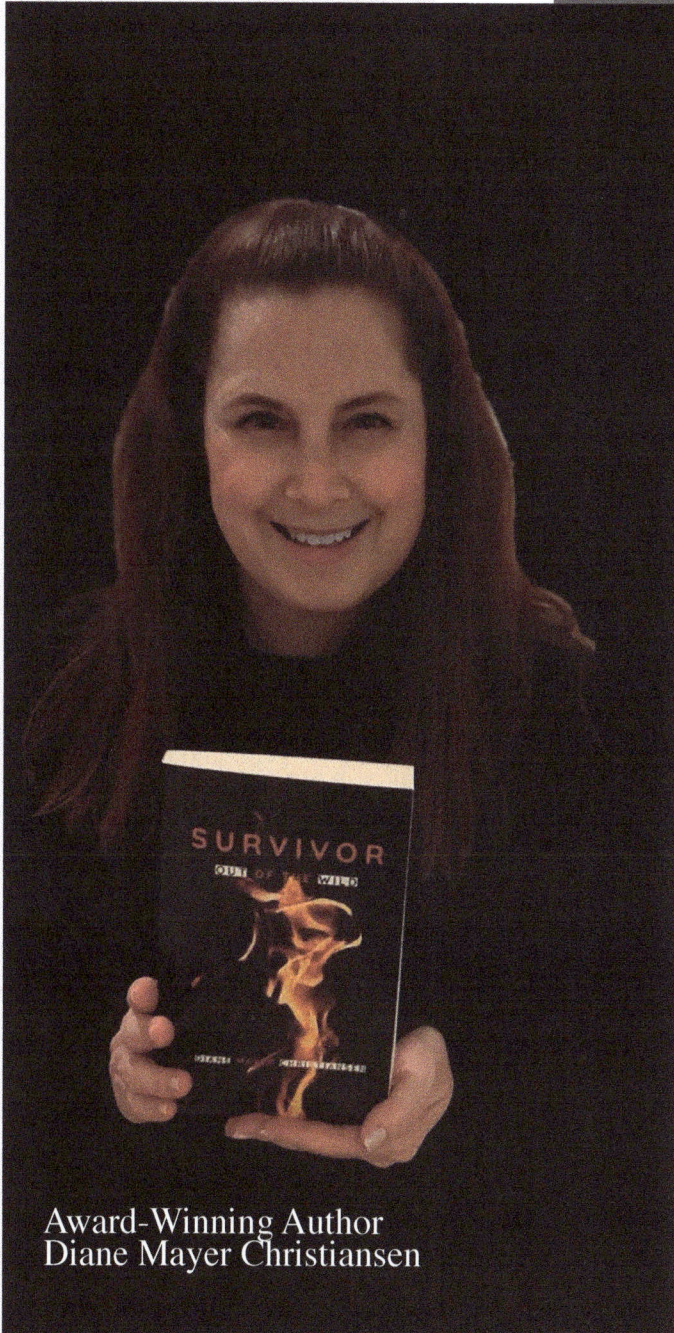

Award-Winning Author
Diane Mayer Christiansen

of positivity around acceptance and disabilities; Diane's purpose-driven vision has come to fruition with the release of Survivor.

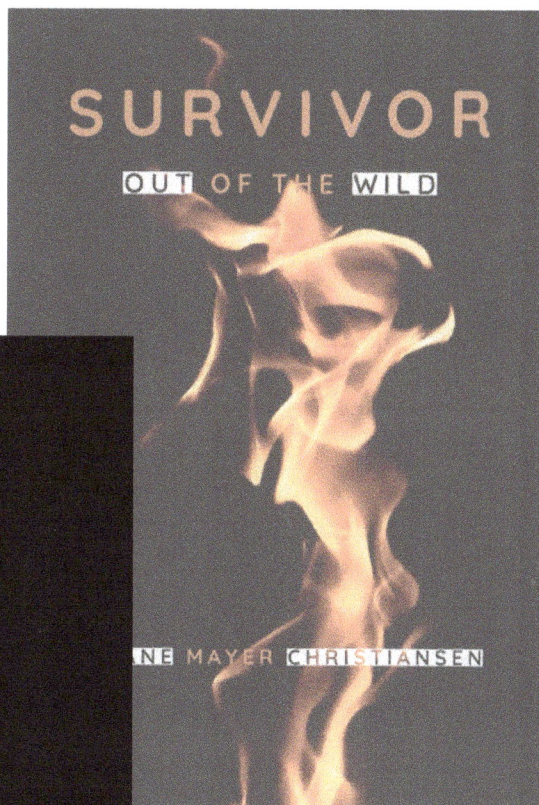

About Diane Mayer Christiansen

Diane Mayer Christiansen is an Award-Winning Author based in Illinois. Growing up in the suburbs of Chicago, Diane struggled immensely with dyslexia, which impacted her ability to read until her late twenties. Determined to rise above her challenges, Diane has dedicated herself to her passion for writing books as a platform for the past decade. Best known for Planet A, an award-winning memoir of Autism Spectrum Disorder, Diane speaks heavily on the topic of Autism from the first-hand experience with her son, Jackie. In her latest novel Survivor: Out of the Wild, Diane explores a post-apocalyptic dystopia, focusing on themes of strength, acceptance, and self-love.

After 3 Months in Coma, COVID Survivor Shares His Near-Death Experience Story

Former 'America's Got Talent' dancer finalist David Paris survives COVID-19 near-death experience. After three months in a coma, he shares his experience, and gives hope to COVID patients and their families, in his new book 'A COVID Story.'

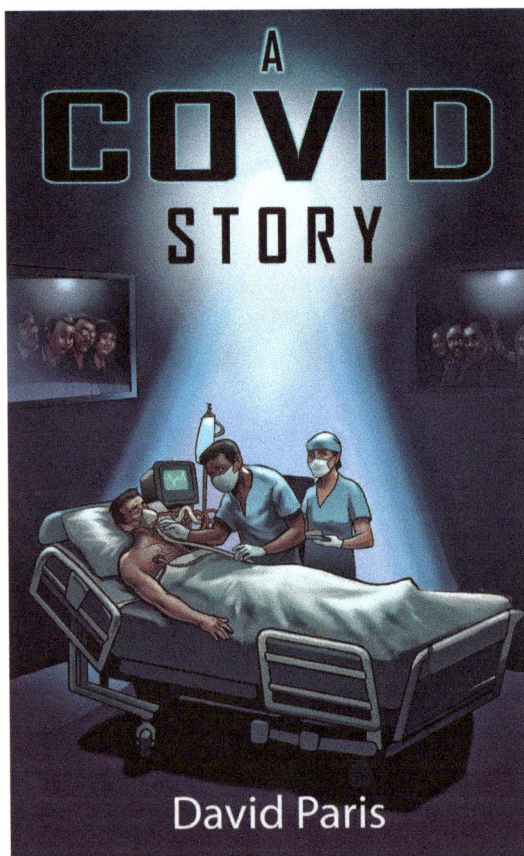

'A COVID Story' by David Paris, front cover.

David Paris Books presents A COVID Story, a heartwarming introspective memoir of an induced medical coma, a unique recovery process, and an amazing community that supported a patient's second chance at life.

After his heart stopped four times during 88 days under acute care and physical therapy, David Paris survived one of the most brutal COVID-19 cases recorded at NYU Langone Health during the 2020 COVID-19 pandemic.

This book offers support for survivors, insights for their caregivers, hope for those currently infected and their families, as well as persuasive evidence for those untouched by COVID's deadly embrace.

The book is a relevant resource including multiple voices sharing insightful perspectives from doctors, nurses, therapists, family, and co-workers. Informative throughout, vibrantly hilarious at times, A COVID Story is written with a heartfelt message of gratitude.

David Paris, author, commented that he hopes "survivors will connect to my experience, caregivers will have a sense of what they can do to help them, and to make COVID more real for those people who have been spared from its devastating impact."

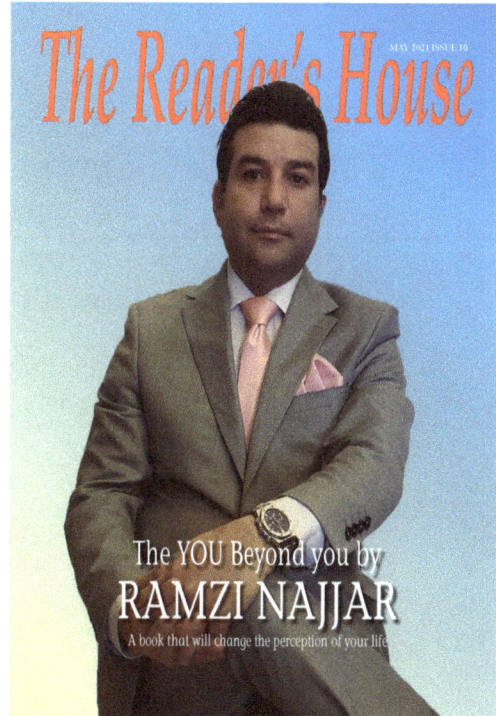

The Reader's House

MAY 2021 ISSUE 16

The YOU Beyond you by
RAMZI NAJJAR

A book that will change the perception of your life

Florence
WILMA ADELMUND-CONRADS

In this Issue

EDITOR'S LETTER

We're so proud to be releasing second updated personalized magazine of The Reader's House that exists to connect writers, authors, artists, musicians, coaches who are always ready to share their story and passion with an interview, and we put them to The Reader's House spotlight.

On our cover is acclaimed Author and spiritual thinker *Ramzi Najjar*, has released a new book, The YOU beyond you, that various authorities have already rewarded.

We have had an ample time to talk about his career and his praised title "The You Beyond You."

We continue to connect people who are always ready to share their story and passion with an interview, and we put them to The Reader's House spotlight. We have interviewed not just acclaimed, as well as award winning authors like *Jennifer Anne Gordon*, a gothic horror/literary fiction novelist, won the Kindle Award for Best Horror/Suspense for 2020, Won Best Horror 2020 from Authors on the Air, was a Finalist for American Book Fest's Best Book Award- Horror, 2020. She also received the Platinum 5 Star Review from Reader's Choice as well as the Gold Seal from Book View.

We featured Enlightened Thought Leader *Dr. Chérie Carter-Scott* on the cover of March issue. *Dr Chérie* is #1 New York Times Best Selling Author (19 Books), Oprah Winfrey Endorsed, Consultant to Fortune 500 companies.

International Bestselling Author *Kathrin Hutson*, NY Times Bestseller Author *Tosca Lee*, Acclaimed crime fiction Canadian Author, *Melissa Yi*, Past President of the Sisters In Crime NJ and Award Winning Author, *Kristina Rienzi* are some of authors we will feature on the cover in upcoming issues.

Enjoy reading,

A. Harlow

The Reader's House

Published by Newyox

LONDON OFFICE
3rd Floor
86-90 Paul Street
London
EC2A 4NE UK

t: +44 20 3828 7097
editor@newyox.com
newyox.com

Due to the current lockdown in England, we are working remotely until further notice.
Currently, we are still producing publications; should this change, we will contact any customers this affects. This means our phones have been turned off and we're currently only available by email (editor@newyox.com). We will be answering emails as quickly as possible and we thank you in advance for your patience and understanding. We'll keep our website updated as and when things change.

Editor in Chief
Anna Harlow
Managing Director
Dan Peters
Marketing Director
Ben Alan

CONTRIBUTORS

Mickey Mikkelson
Andy Machin
Rocky Cole
Jean Taylor
Rosina S Khan
Shalini M
Anders Abadie
Vinod Vullikanti
Hannah SPRAKER

The YOU Beyond you by
RAMZI NAJJAR
A book that will change the perception of your life

The You Beyond You takes readers on a journey through both the seen and unseen toxicity of our modern environment. It deals with both mental and physical assaults on the minds and body. And it gives users what Najjar hopes will be liberating tools.

BY DAN PETERS
April 15, 2021

Author and spiritual thinker Ramzi Najjar has released a new book, The YOU beyond you, that various authorities have already rewarded. These are;
• Literary Titan's Silver Award for Best Book - December 5, 2020
• Pinnacle Book Achievement Award for Best Body/Mind/Spirit Book - December 15, 2020
• Finalist Foreword Indies Awards - March 12, 2021 - Final Results June 17, 2021
"The Knowledge of the Willing" will help readers navigate the modern world's environmental, emotional, and spiritual challenges. It contains secrets that Najjar hopes will allow his audience to live more fruitfully and healthily under challenging times. The book explores and challenges our society's norms and shows readers that there are fundamentally different ways of being.

The You Beyond You takes readers on a journey through both the seen and unseen toxicity of our modern environment. It deals with both mental and physical assaults on the minds and body. And it gives users what Najjar hopes will be liberating tools. "We always experience life through our subjective perceptions, built-up beliefs, and what we have been taught or told by others and seldomly stop to meditate on the reality which surrounds us." Says the Award-Winning Author Ramzi Najjar and underlined that "Most of our beliefs and perceptions today is rather a collection of misleading ideas due to the many blockages and diversions in our lives, that hinder to a great extent our understanding of our true Reality. This enlightened guide offers the reader a method to dissolve all that we acquire as bad habits, beliefs, and energies that have been gathered through experiences and passive knowledge and unlock a new dimension of Reality by applying concepts, principles, and givens never heard of before."

Continued *on page 16*

"
We always experience life through our subjective perceptions, built-up beliefs, and what we have been taught or told by others and seldomly stop to meditate on the reality which surrounds us."
--Ramzi Najjar

5 Strategies to
Earn Money
on the Internet

The selling of e-books has a lot of benefits within the sale of physical items along with even the supply of numerous solutions. You may avoid spending money and time by giving e books twenty-four hours per day, 7 days a week, and automate your own business to suit you.

By Jean Taylor

With so many new online business chances, it's tricky to filter the audience. Maybe your venture capital is quite tiny. Since you are at present working outside, you may have minimal period for you to begin out your organization at the beginning. Probably you are interested in an internet business that isn't hard to control and will not require too much worry. If every one of these pertains to a situation, subsequently attempting to sell an eBook could be right for you personally.

Thousands of people earn extra money by purchasing eBooks or enjoying full time business at home. E-books can be purchased wherever you get on the web, covering a wide array of subjects, ranging from cooking into decor in your home and economic information. With internet charge card processing, they are simple to buy and can be readily read and downloaded. The great thing about the eBook business is you do not possess an inventory you may keep up with, no overhead for generating eBooks (if you don't spend your time writing eBooks) and that you also don't have transportation troubles. The selling of e-books has a lot of benefits within the sale of physical items along with even the supply of numerous solutions. You may avoid spending money and time by giving e books twenty-four hours per day, 7 days a week, and automate your own business to suit you. Start hunting on the web for eBook opportunities today and that means you're able to achieve your aims as speedily as you possibly can. We will explore five ways to produce money on the internet by offering eBooks.

1.Let the others sell e-books

Yet another way to create money on the internet through e-books is always to let the others sell e-books. You can provide rights or commissions into eBooks and aid others create new on-line organizations. When you help others generate income online, you'll even receive rewards. E-books are easy to market to their intentions and can be readily sent to many others for sale. Inch. Teach others to market eBooks.

2.Boost E Books through different online tools

Once you opt to offer some e books, it is the right time to promote them. For any new internet organization, you wish to start with an excellent site and an effective sales presentation. Without these, you will not be able to change traffic to paying customers, which means that your audience will be in vain. In the event you are not really a writer, employ a professional sales writer to create a backup for you. After, when you offer e-books such as spicy cakes, the money is worth it! If you promote numerous eBooks, then don't forget to set up a presentation for every single

respective book. This provides you with a much-increased impact on search engines like Google and assist you to target your own readers.

3. Choose and opt for that appeal you

The real key to good results would be to develop a solid firm when selling the products which interest you. Do you want to simply help others throughout financing or allow them to get out of the debt? Sale of e-books linked to fund. Do you like to produce crafts? Market electronic books. Are you really an expert fisherman? Provide

> The real key to good results would be to develop a solid firm when selling the products which interest you. Do you want to simply help others throughout financing or allow them to get out of the debt? Sale of e-books linked to fund. Do you like to produce crafts? Market electronic books.

information on fishing in books. This listing has been moving on, so you may earn money online and perform something that you really like!

4. Read e-books

You must completely understand the goods you market. If you really don't write your own eBook, make sure to see the eBook you provided. This can permit one to answer consumer requirements, compose effective sales demonstrations, and provide readers with information concerning eBooks. Attempting to sell matters, you think will be much simpler, and you also ought to ensure the caliber of the situations you present would be your idea. If you blindly sell somebody else's e-book without reading, it will hinder your capability to generate money on the web. Once you've set up your site, commence sending all your webpages for the main search engine. This can be done through the search engine marketing pro-

motion corporation or you can do it yourself. Then look for opportunities for pay-per-click search engines and that means that you can target traffic. Pay per click permits you to choose and choose which keywords to target. Your site will only appear in search results if you employ those specific keywords and phrases. You can cover a little charge for each click; however, a lot of your customers will soon be enthusiastic about your goods. Other efficient types of on-line advertisements include press announcements, Magazine advertisements (or newsletters), classified ads, auctions, and shopping centers. You may publish your own e-book, hire somebody to compose a letter or sign a deal with a business which delivers the right to market eBooks. If you utilize electronic guides from different companies, this will help you save you headaches and time. You can even choose an e-book to promote. Then you can certainly only offer to the people who are interested.

5. Purchase of Ad-On merchandise to profit e-book clients

After you begin selling eBooks and creating a customer base, you could promote. You can offer products in your e-books via affiliate hyperlinks. Or, you may be offering a fresh e-book to an earlier purchased customer. In the event you want to offer you a service apart from the purchase of electronic books, you may use an electronic publication to get a buyer base. Then you can present your primary service.

Visit https://www.makemoneyonlinehappy.com for FREE e-books and tips about making money online.

Article Source: EzineArticles

Wuthering Heights (Deluxe Edition)

by EMILY BRONTË

ISBN: 978-1641814140
PUBLISHER: iBoo Press House

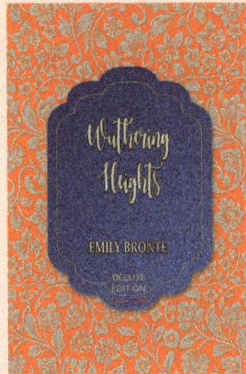

Wuthering Heights is a novel by Emily Brontë published in 1847 under her pseudonym "Ellis Bell". Brontë's only finished novel, it was written between October 1845 and June 1846. Wuthering Heights and Anne Brontë's Agnes Grey were accepted by publisher Thomas Newby before the success of her sister Charlotte's novel Jane Eyre. After Emily's death, Charlotte edited a posthumous second edition in 1850.

Although Wuthering Heights is now a classic of English literature, contemporaneous reviews were deeply polarised; it was controversial because of its unusually stark depiction of mental and physical cruelty, and it challenged Victorian ideas about religion, morality, class and woman's place in society. The English poet and painter Dante Gabriel Rossetti, although an admirer of the book, referred to it as "A fiend of a book - an incredible monster [...] The action is laid in hell, - only it seems places and people have English names there."

Wuthering Heights was influenced by Romanticism including the novels of Walter Scott, gothic fiction, and Byron, and the moorland setting is significant.

The novel has inspired many adaptations, including film, radio and television dramatisations; a musical; a ballet; operas; and a hit song.

"This novel is an incredible achievement by a young girl who dared to become an author !" Barnes & Noble Customer.

Fear and Longing in Los Angeles

by MARK LESLIE

ISBN: 978-1989351222
PUBLISHER: Stark Publishing

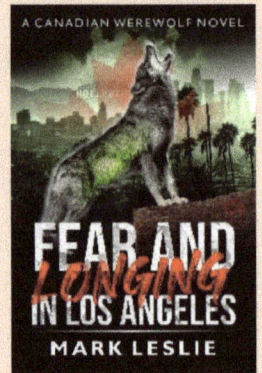

If New York is the city that never sleeps, then L.A. is the city where you have to sleep with one eye open. Michael Andrews learns quickly that it's not just the cut-throat world of Hollywood you need to be leery of. There's something deeper, darker, and far more disturbing lurking beneath the surface of the city, operating in the shadows and striking at the most vulnerable.
An extended trip to Los Angeles to be on set for the movie adaptation of his latest novel leads Michael into a world of glamour and fear. He becomes entangled with an intriguing, sexy, and mysterious woman. At times she seems just what he needs in order to finally get over the unrequited love of his ex-girlfriend; but at other times, her presence appears to be the gateway to a Pandora's box of B-movie nightmares.
Can Michael trust her with his secret? Can he trust himself with her?
Michael's supernatural wolf-enhanced powers and special abilities might not be enough to survive this harsh and gritty jungle and the long tentacles of white supremacy that have long lurked beneath the surface, waiting for the right time to make themselves known.

"He's a successful author and a minor celebrity living in Manhattan. It's a pretty big step up from his humble Canadian upbringing. Of course, his lycanthropy poses a bit of a challenge.' For those in doubt, a lycanthrope is a human with the ability to shapeshift into a wolf – aka 'werewolf.' Mark adds that Michael Andrews is 'a meek and mild-mannered person, not cut out for the hero life – an Alpha Wolf who is really a Beta Human.' Grady Harp

Dammit ... It IS Menopause
by SALLY BARTLETT

Pub Date: Nov. 22, 2020
PUBLISHER: Ginger Books Press

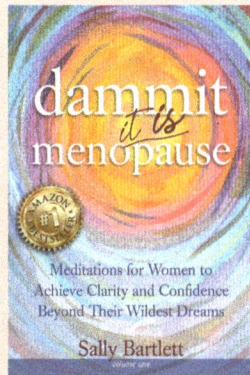

Sally Bartlett, author of "Dammit ... It IS Menopause! Meditations for Women to Achieve Clarity and Confidence Beyond Their Wildest Dreams, Volume 1," ranked No. 1 Bestseller in ten categories on Amazon last Friday. The categories included Menopause, Women's Health, Meditation, Self-Help, Aging, Heart Disease, Humor Essays, Weight Loss Maintenance, Twelve-Step Programs, and Diabetic & Sugar-Free Cookbooks. The book was launched with volume two in January, 2021.
"Dammit ... It IS Menopause!" is a collection of journal entries written over a 15-year period while Bartlett was experiencing menopause symptoms including hot flashes, memory problems, weight gain, depression, anxiety and insomnia. The book is described by the author as an intimate and candid look behind the scenes of what many women experience during this phase of their life. It was written with the intent to offer hope and encouragement to women suffering with similar symptoms.
"What started as a way to survive my negative self-talk and the way I felt about my changing body became a collection of inspirational daily meditations. During perimenopause, I felt terribly alone and feared I was losing my mind. Through a number of self-loving practices — physical, intellectual, emotional and spiritual — I learned to embrace the transition and thrive. I overcame disordered and emotional eating, quit dieting and made peace with my weight and food. I share my poignant, yet humorous, writings with other women so they too can learn to love their body and their life," said Bartlett.
Bartlett's fan base refers to her as the dean of varsity menopause, a title she gave herself after attending her son's college orientation. It was there that the dean of students explained that a dean's job was to provide support for a successful navigation during a season of life. This concept resonated with Bartlett as she offers guidance to women during perimenopause and beyond.
Bartlett further commented, "Why varsity? Varsity is a term coined by one of my close friends when I wanted her recognition for completing some small task like cleaning out the vegetable bin in my refrigerator. She played along and proclaimed, 'that's Varsity.' It just stuck. What a wonderful, universal way to celebrate each other!"

THE NICKEL BOYS
by Colson Whitehead

Pub Date: July 16th, 2019
ISBN: 978-0-385-53707-0

KIRKUS REVIEW
The acclaimed author of The Underground Railroad (2016) follows up with a leaner, meaner saga of Deep South captivity set in the mid-20th century and fraught with horrors more chilling for being based on true-life atrocities.
Elwood Curtis is a law-abiding, teenage paragon of rectitude, an avid reader of encyclopedias and after-school worker diligently overcoming hardships that come from being abandoned by his parents and growing up black and poor in segregated Tallahassee, Florida. It's the early 1960s, and Elwood can feel changes coming every time he listens to an LP of his hero Martin Luther King Jr. sermonizing about breaking down racial barriers. But while hitchhiking to his first day of classes at a nearby black college, Elwood accepts a ride in what turns out to be a stolen car and is sentenced to the Nickel Academy, a juvenile reformatory that looks somewhat like the campus he'd almost attended but turns out to be a monstrously racist institution whose students, white and black alike, are brutally beaten, sexually abused, and used by the school's two-faced officials to steal food and supplies. At first, Elwood thinks he can work his way past the arbitrary punishments and sadistic treatment ("I am stuck here, but I'll make the best of it…and I'll make it brief"). He befriends another black inmate, a street-wise kid he knows only as Turner, who has a different take on withstanding Nickel: "The key to in here is the same as surviving out there—you got to see how people act, and then you got to figure out how to get around them like an obstacle course." And if you defy them, Turner warns, you'll get taken "out back" and are never seen or heard from again. Both Elwood's idealism and Turner's cynicism entwine into an alliance that compels drastic action—and a shared destiny. Inspired by disclosures of a real-life Florida reform school's long-standing corruption and abusive practices, Whitehead's novel displays its author's facility with violent imagery and his skill at weaving narrative strands into an ingenious, if disquieting whole.
There's something a tad more melodramatic in this book's conception (and resolution) than one expects from Whitehead, giving it a drugstore-paperback glossiness that enhances its blunt-edged impact.

← **Continued** *from page 10*

Please tell us about yourself?

I was born in Beit Mery, a small town located in Mount Lebanon, Lebanon, in 1978, I spent most of my childhood in a time of war. From an early age, I experienced immense stress growing up amidst the Lebanese civil war, where I witness all kinds of destruction, explosions, and bombings. I started to find ways to alleviate this kind of pressure and stress by contemplating the other side of life at a very young age.

At the my age of 12, the war ended.

tancy.

A year later, in 2019, I became a partner at Libonsai, the first Botanical Garden, Green Museum, and Bonsai Cedar Reserve in Lebanon. In the same year, I established AmmenOnline, a platform that offers direct motor insurance coverage.

In 2020, I released my book - The YOU beyond you, a self-help. and motivational book related to personal transformation and spirituality that offers some new concepts on the nature of our Reality

In 2021, I enter into a distribution agreement with Anecdote Publishing

beyond you - The knowledge of the Willing," which is a summary of what I believe Reality is and how it works.

It is a praised book and you already get some awards after your book released. What is "The YOU beyond you." Please tell us about it?

"The YOU beyond you" contains the most logical explanation for the real secrets of our existence and how they operate within us and in our environment. This process occurs right before our eyes, yet we are mostly unable to notice it due to many obstructions and diversions in our lives. The book is a must-read of at least once in a lifetime for everyone willing to experience our Reality's real dynamics and go beyond the limited norms. The book describes life's forces at work, which one can use as a platform to unveil his full knowledge and his true potentials.

No matter who we are or our life goal, our bad habits, and unhealthy beliefs are the only reasons that trouble us in becoming the best versions of ourselves.

"The You beyond you' is a rather challenging read, which makes one start re-evaluating one's life even if the reader had no intention of doing so." Diana Levit

However, I remained stuck in comparing the chaos that ruled before to the calm and serenity that resulted from post-war.

I always wondered why people get so aggressive at times, and at other times, they were friendly and living in total peace. I used to attend school, but my main interests were all subjects not taught at school, like the nature of the Reality we live in and people's psychologies, and what makes people act the way they do.

I completed my college education at Louise Wegmann College.

I went to the American University of Beirut in 1997, where I pursued a bachelor's degree in Political Science and Public Administration.

When I was 24, after completing my one-year mandatory military service, I decides to travel to Kuwait to start my career due to my country's lack of opportunities. That allowed me more time with myself and allowed me to discover the power in silence and solitude.

How about your career

In 2012 I founded Securita , an insurance firm headquartered in Kuwait with operations in the Middle East and across the Gulf region.

In 2018, I founded Securita Re, a sister firm of Securita, that specializes in reinsurance broking and consul-

in India for The YOU beyond you.

Could you tell us about Personal Transformation and Spirituality?

I realized the importance of "Accumulation" in life from an early age and that everything either associates to form a more significant entity or

dissociates to vanish in Reality.

One day in 2013, sitting in my office trying to relieve work stress, I was watching the news on the TV like usual. I say I experienced a sort of thunder hitting me, a kind of awakening resulting in an intense headache for a full day.

I could not continue the way I was unconsciously living, and I need to apply consciousness and filtering to all that I do.

Filtering all that comes in my life, from food to thoughts to social interactions, my reality started to change into a more enlightened existential living.

In 2020, the lockdowns due to COVID-19 created the time needed to put all my life realizations and knowledge into my book "The YOU

"The YOU Beyond You, by Ramzi Najjar, provides a much-needed wake up call for anyone looking for an answer to life's many difficulties." Benjamin W.

In this book, you will embark on thorough research on how these bad habits and chaotic knowledge get embedded in our life system and create a negative framework for our lives. The book's knowledge will set readers on an attitude that lets them consciously and unconsciously break free from these limitations and experience the proper path where everything prospers.

Who should read this book?

It covers practically every dimension of life, from one's frame of mind to metaphysics. And it highlights the mental habits people consciously and unconsciously adopt, providing a much-needed roadmap for how to escape them.

This book is a guide for readers of

all ages, entailing every dimension of our Reality. A demonstration of what makes and breaks life. Written with the sole purpose of assisting the reader in understanding how mind, body, and soul work within our environment and how these age-old beliefs and perceptions which we accumulated can be turned around, dissolved, or turned into a directed drive to flourish.

So, whoever is ready to unveil life's real secrets, overcome obstacles in their way of thinking, and step out of their comfort zones to grow and succeed, is advised to read it.

The book is inspired by biological and psychological theories, ideas, and true-life experiences. It is a comprehensive guide that provides you with an extraordinary life approach to reach new heights.

What are the essential points that you underline for your book?

able to overcome the thoughts that frame our minds and destroy mental peace. And they would have a much better understanding of the dynamics that form our Reality. Ultimately, I

"What better time to turn towards yourself and do some soul searching than the middle of a pandemic? It can be daunting, nearly overwhelming, to consider all that make you who you are, but The You Beyond You by Ramzi Najjar is definitely the best place to get started on your journey. " Sarah Jayne

want the work to empower people, allowing readers to take control of their lives, both for the betterment of themselves and others. The goal is to guide readers towards a state of spiritual enlightenment - a form of sustained bliss and levity. That, in my view, is a path to a better world.

You say that "people need to stay motivated to survive." How do you stay motivated?

"The author has a wonderful way of getting right to the point, but in a way that is comprehensive and applicable.. " Katrina, Amazon Reviewer

After reading this book, you will be enlightened on:
• How a multitude of habits pollutes our bodies.
• How to overcome thoughts and ideas that frame our minds.
• How to eliminate factors that destroy mental peace.
• How to take control and improve ourselves and the environment around us for self-betterment.
• How to experience the real secrets of life and understand how they operate.
• How to be able to use these concepts to bind Reality in your way.
• How to reach spiritual awakening

What are the benefits of reading this book for readers?

After reading the book, readers should better understand the mental habits that are "polluting [their] bodies. They should also be better

Well, motivation alone is not sufficient. One can be motivated all the time but reach no place. You can compare motivation to a muscle car. If you have a bad driver behind the wheel, the experience will generate chaos. Before being motivated, one should filter all negativity acquired from the outside by avoiding putting himself in unpleasant scenarios or situations and reasoning his actions and reactions, thus implementing a system where he uses his consciousness in everything he does. We need to be proactive in acquiring knowledge and not let data in, in a passive manner. I have removed TV, news, harmful social interactions, and all sorts of data that can unconsciously get to my mind by totally avoiding being exposed to them.

Once this is in place, you can put a clear vision for your life, and the lack of demotivators can leave space for motivation which allows you to di-

rect your energy towards productive goals. Remove all harmful data from what surrounds you, and your mind and thoughts will be automatically shifting towards productivity.

You stated that the majority of what we know is only partial. What advice would you give to someone who is struggling to come to terms with that?

Yes, I believe all that we know and all that we could ever know, no matter how ample it is, would remain partial in nature, and this is because we as humans are just a tiny fragment of the Reality we live in, and our brains can only read a limited spectrum of it. The way to deal with that is to always take this as a constant and never have rigid beliefs in life, leading to aggressiveness and mind-blocks.

Knowing that our knowledge is partial in any subject should always lead to more lenient social interactions. Moreover, one should work daily on segregating these partial realities in his life and understand what to allow in and what not to. As soon as this task is achieved, more clarity would follow. That is a strength and not a weakness, as if our knowledge was stiff and complete, our humanity would be stagnant with little room for development. However, the key is in putting this partial information together and what we build with them.

Do you plan to write more books on this same subject?

Yes, this was the tip of the iceberg. I intend to write a second book explaining more in-depth the dynamics I communicated to readers in The YOU beyond you – The knowledge of the willing. ●

Everyone has heard of antioxidants, and their various benefits for our skin, but don't actually know what these antioxidants are, or what they do.

In the fight against free radicals, the molecules that damage the different components of our skin's cell (DNA, Proteins and outer barrier), antioxidants are proven to be extremely beneficial. As naturally occurring vitamins, antioxidants help neutralize these free radicals thereby keeping them contained. With this and many other benefits such as brightened skin and reduced hyperpigmentation in mind, skincare with antioxidants is considered a must have today.

The Super Power of Antioxidants

Different vitamins offer different benefits when added to skincare regimes. Some of the most commonly used vitamins in skincare are vitamins A, C, E, and F.

Vitamin A – A widely used vitamin in skincare is Vitamin A, which is known for its anti-ageing properties. You'll find this antioxidant in the name of retinol in skincare (retinol is the concentrated version of this vitamin). Retinol is known to fill wrinkles, smoothen fine lines and rough patches on the skin. It is also commonly used to combat severe acne, by decreasing inflammation, controlling excess sebum production, evening out skin tones and increasing cell growth to heal acne scarring.

Vitamin C – For skin that is dull and needs brightening, Vitamin C is the ultimate antioxidant. With results showing after 6-8 weeks of continuous use, this vitamin is responsible for lightening dark spots and reducing hyperpigmentation, resulting in bright and glowing skin.

Vitamin E – For moisturising benefits, one of the more commonly used antioxidants is Vitamin E. The gentle but effective vitamin has anti-inflammatory properties and anti-ageing properties, all while maintaining elasticity and keeping skin soft. Its gentle nature allows for it to be used synergistically with other antioxidants. That's why you'll find a lot of Vitamins C and E combined skincare products in the market!

Vitamin F – For skin that seems dry and dull, but is also acne prone, Vitamin F is the way to go. Vitamin F represents linoleic acid, which is a fatty acid rich in omega-6. These fats (also known as lipids) are extremely important to maintain a healthy skin barrier.

MZ Skin Tone & Lift Roller is made with germanium, a key ingredient in activating and balancing the positive and negative ions responsible for ageing, while simultaneously defending skin from surrounding environmental aggressors.

How To
Look Like
A Top
Model

By Vinod Vullikanti

odeling is perceived as if it is a representation or a "certification" of superiority in appearance because not everyone can become a model. Being a model impresses people and because of this, there are actually many people who will light up at the thought of being a model. As such, this article will be to help those who aspire to be a model, but do not know how to get started.

1) Know the kind of model you want to become

There are various forms of models, from runway models to commercial models, event models, blogshop models, photo models et cetera. People tend to generalize the term "models", meaning they associate models solely as runway models, which is obviously not the case. You need to know what kind of model you want to become before you set your sights to becoming one. For example, if you are tall, have sharp facial features and a slim body, you might want to try to be a runway model. If you are good at socializing and grooming yourself, you can try out event modeling. There are many different options, but be sure to find out which one suits you best.

2) Finding a modeling agency

In order to kick start your career in modeling, there are various different ways. Like promoting yourself on social media, blog posts and even joining competitions. However, the best and the most direct way of becoming a model is to join a modeling agency. Modeling agencies have many different clients, and therefore they are able to provide you the best clients and assignments that suit your needs. However, most modeling agencies will require you to pay a premium, which can range from hundreds to thousands of dollars. The money paid will be used to create a portfolio, which includes having professional photographers take photos of you and creating a composite card. The modeling agencies will then send your composite card to clients who will then review and see if you are suitable to be their model for their project. The main thing to note is, while all agencies will have their own client base,

not all agencies have many clients. Meaning to say, you have to do your research and find out the agencies which have many different clients. That way, it increases your chance of securing projects, otherwise, you could be left in the cold after paying the fee.

3) Understand the trend of modeling

The modeling industry is not very huge, though it is getting better. Unfortunately, not everyone can make it big by simply modeling. Meaning to say, you should not rely solely on modeling to earn a living. Yes, it could be a path to joining showbiz like Mediacorp, but it is not very common. In the world, Caucasians are preferred to Asians for modeling. They are generally taller or have better features and proportions, while Asians cannot really hold a candle beside them. Of course I am not saying for everyone, hope you do not misunderstand.
All in all, if you dare to dream, dare to try out, you stand a chance. You never know what will happen if you do not try. Do your research, get your mind and body ready, like grooming yourself and maintaining a healthy diet, and you will realize that your dream is not far away.
Wondering how to get into modeling? Getting Started as a Model. iModels Holdings is the leading model agency in Singapore.

Source:EzineArticles

The best and the most direct way of becoming a model is to join a modeling agency. Modeling agencies have many different clients, and therefore they are able to provide you the best clients and assignments that suit your needs.

Charles Marquez's New Book
'BLT: Blessed Lucky Tenacious'

is an Intriguing Assessment of the Times and the Author's Opinion on the Preservation of Life

Charles Marquez's New Book 'BLT: Blessed Lucky Tenacious' is an Intriguing Assessment of the Times and the Author's Opinion on the Preservation of Life

Charles Marquez, a former U.S. Army officer (New Mexico National Guard; former New Mexico state senator, 1980–1984; former Foreign Service Officer, Department of State, Washington, D.C.), with tours in Colombia, South America, and Toronto, Canada, has completed his most recent book "BLT: Blessed Lucky Tenacious": a thought-provoking and opinion-based look at the issues of global war and the preservation of life.

Published by Fulton Books, Charles Marquez's book details a situation in Colombia at the American Consulate, where the author was serving as a vice-consul. He was able to obtain the release of a U.S. citizen from a Colombian prison and probably saved his life. While Mr. Marquez adhered to protocol, he also established quid pro quo or reciprocity— far more effective than protocol. It was reciprocity that allowed the release of the U.S. citizen and what made Mr. Marquez more effective in Colombia.

Charles Marquez firmly believes in the preservation of all lives, including the innocent unborn. He also strongly affirms that global peace is possible by the restructuring of the United Nations, ulti-

BLT

LESSED LUCKY TENACIOUS

CHARLES MARQUEZ

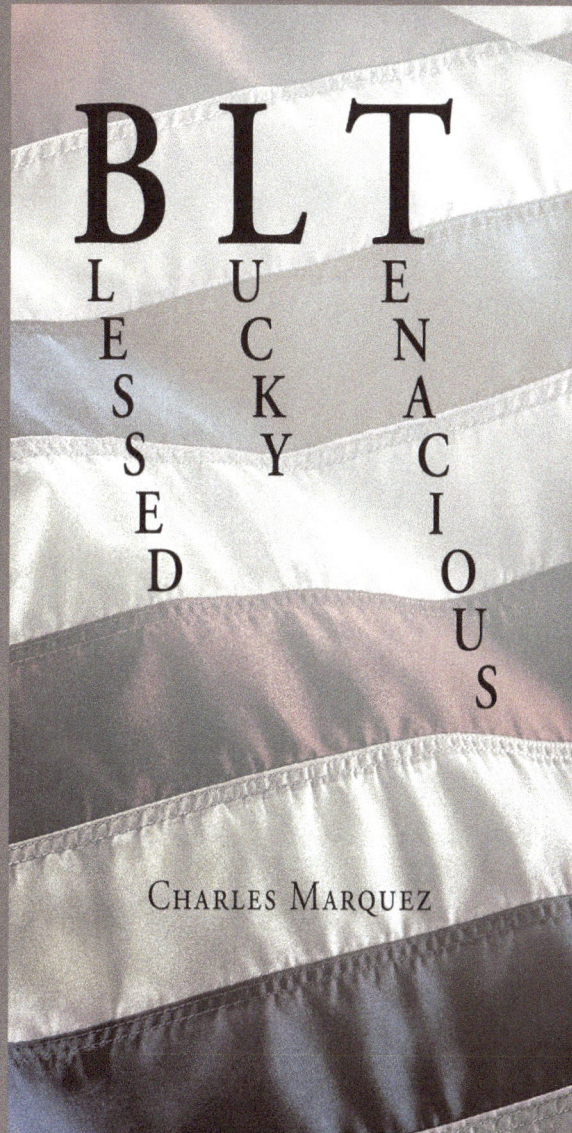

mately preventing warfare, rather than futile attempts to
remedy those situations. All things are possible and can
be attained with the appropriate application of discipline
and ethical behavior.

Readers who wish to experience this inspired work can
purchase "BLT: Blessed Lucky Tenacious" at bookstores
everywhere, or online at the Apple iTunes Store, Amazon,
Google Play or Barnes & Noble.

For Artist

4

TIPS

How to Find a Talent Agency
Find out what type of Model you are.

Depending on your age, height and weight, certain agencies specialize in working with specific type of talent. If you are under the age of 16, you are considered a teen model. Most teen models book catalog or print work in local markets.

Go to Agencies Directly:

There are a lot of modeling agencies out there so the first option you have is to track them down and find them yourself. Unfortunately, one of the biggest issues you have with this is that there are thousands of agencies out there and it can be hard to determine which ones are legit and which ones are just wasting your time. At the same time, getting into a big agency by yourself can be a difficult task, especially if you don't know anyone.

First, find out what type of Model you are:

Depending on your age, height and weight, certain agencies specialize in working with specific type of talent.

If you are under the age of 16, you are considered a teen model. Most teen models book catalog or print work in local markets.
For high fashion models, also know as editorial, are required to be at least 5 Feet 9 inches for woman and at least 6 feet 1 Inch for males. The industry is mostly made up of print or commercial talent, which are commonly booked for household and lifestyle brands. Commercial print work is very lucrative.
Plus size modeling has become increasing popular as most top agencies now have divisions specializing in full-figured talent. To be considered plus size. sizes for female models start at size 8 and up Like commercial modeling, plus

IMAGE: PEXELS

sized modeling and acting is very lucrative as most agents only represent a few in their divisions.

Modeling Scouts:

Another option to find a modeling agent or agency is to go through a scout. As the name suggests, modeling scouts go around the country and try to find models and usually get some kind of fee for bringing new talent to an agency or directly to an agent. Just like with going to an agent directly, though, not all modeling scouts are reputable so you run the risk of wasting your time.

Online Social Media Marketing:

Most models and actors are going online to market themselves to modeling agents and talent scouts. While exposure is key in the entertainment business, social media posting does not allow a model or actor to direct the attention strictly to industry professionals. For new models or actors just starting out in the entertainment business, online posting of certain content may be prohibited by their full-time employer so it is always to best to try to contact agencies or scouts directly.

Latitude Talent Studios has contacts with the most influential modeling and acting agencies in the entertainment business. Additionally, Latitude Talent can help connect models directly and find opportunities with companies like VH1, NBC and HBO. If you are trying to figure out how to find modeling agencies, contact Latitude online at http://www.latitudetalent.com

Source:EzineArticles.com

For Ballet

The Story of the Nutcracker Ballet
The Nutcracker ballet originated from a fairytale written in 1816 by Ernst Theodor Amadeus Hoffmann.

The Nutcracker ballet opens in a quaint German village on Christmas Eve. Townspeople are bustling, getting ready to attend a party at the Stahlbaum home. The members of the Stahlbaum family and their servants are preparing for the holiday celebration.

By Anders Abadie

The Nutcracker ballet originated from a fairytale written in 1816 by Ernst Theodor Amadeus Hoffmann. Although this story was classified as a fairytale, the original plot was not written for children. Years later, Alexander Dumas rewrote the saga with youngsters in mind. Then, in 1892, Peter Tchaikovsky was asked to compose the music for the story. This was the beginning of the popular ballet that has become synonymous with the Christmas holidays.

Act One

The Nutcracker ballet opens in a quaint German village on Christmas Eve. Townspeople are bustling, getting ready to attend a party at the Stahlbaum home. The members of the Stahlbaum family and their servants are preparing for the holiday celebration. As guests arrive, the children, Clara and Fritz, enjoy mingling with their friends. Soon, Clara's godfather, Herr Drosselmeier arrives. Drosselmeier is a local toymaker, and he comes bearing gifts. He passes around the China dolls for the girls and brass bugles for the boys. Fritz receives a charming drum, and Clara receives a beautiful nutcracker. Unfortunately, Fritz becomes jealous of his sister's gift. He seizes it, and promptly breaks it. Drosselmeier saves the day by fixing the broken gift with a wave of his magic handkerchief.

IMAGE: PEXEL

The party breaks up, and Clara fashions a bed for the nutcracker beneath the Christmas tree. After her family goes to bed, the girl sneaks down to check on her new toy one last time. She ends up falling asleep in the parlor with her toy clutched in her arms. At midnight, Clara awakens to startling events. It seems that she has shrunken to the size of her toys. An army of mice led by a menacing Mouse King is threatening the toys. The nutcracker gathers other soldiers and a battle ensues. At one point it seems that the Mouse King will prevail, but then Clara intervenes and throws her slipper at the Mouse King. After receiving a blow to the head, the king succumbs, and his army carries him away. The girl falls asleep once again after the excitement ends.

Act Two

When the youngster awakens the next time, she is in a forest on her way to the Kingdom of Snow. The nutcracker is now a prince, and the two are en route to the Land of Sweets. When they arrive, the Sugar Plum Fairy greets them and asks them to stay for a special festival. Next, the citizens of the Land of Sweets begin performing various dances for them. Different characters take the stage to perform lavishly for their guests. Finally, the Sugar Plum Fairy herself takes the stage with the Cavalier to perform the legendary Pas de Deux. After a grand finale, the two guests are ready to leave. Clara wakes on Christmas morning with the nutcracker still in her arms. Her dream is a dim memory, but she still has her beloved toy to treasure. Anyone fortunate enough to see the Nutcracker ballet live will come away with visions of sugar plums and fairies in their eyes.

To learn more about their options for seeing the Nutcracker ballet, Boston residents should visit http://ballettheatre.org.

Source: EzineArticles

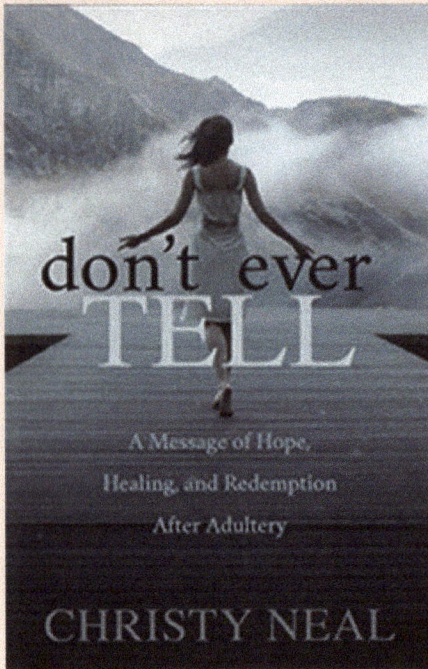

"Through its message of forgiveness and hope, 'Don't Ever Tell' helps women make peace with their past and save their marriages." — Christy Neal

New Christian Marriage Book by Christy Neal Helps Women Find Healing for Infidelity

NASHVILLE, TN, US, February 24, 2021 /EINPresswire.com/ -- Morgan James' new release, "Don't Ever Tell: A Message of Hope, Healing, and Redemption After Adultery," by Christy Neal, is the brave story of one woman who engaged in sexual immorality, faced her transgressions, and found light after the darkness. Don't Ever Tell helps women who have had an affair move on from their past and discover the forgiveness that awaits them.

In "Don't Ever Tell: A Message of Hope, Healing, and Redemption After Adultery," Christy Neal shares the haunting story of Scarlett, a Christian woman struggling with infidelity. As an unlikely character to engage in an affair, Scarlett, a sweet, unsuspecting Southern girl, embodies the truth that anyone is susceptible to sin. As Christy Neal depicts the darkest moments of Scarlett's life, women will become emotionally invested in her journey from hopelessness and despair to redemption and healing.
Christy Neal's personal experiences

shape the direction of her writing. She knows deeply and personally the burden that sexual sin casts on women who commit it and hopes that her words will inspire others to trade judgment for compassion as they reach out to individuals in need.

Deeply transparent, raw, and gut-wrenching, "Don't Ever Tell: A Message of Hope, Healing, and Redemption After Adultery" candidly explores the taboo topic of adultery in Christian women, providing a safe place to discuss an issue that so many silently struggle with. Through its message of forgiveness and hope, "Don't Ever Tell" helps women make peace with their pasts and save their marriages.

If you would like more information about this topic, or to schedule an interview with Christy Neal, please contact authorsupport@morgan-jamespublishing.com.

About the Author:
Christy Neal is an advocate for women who feel tainted and cast out after adultery. As the author of "Don't Ever Tell" and the podcast host of "Everyone Has A Voice," Christy is now the catalyst for healing she desperately needed but never found over a decade ago after her own affair. She has been featured on Zebras and Cheetahs with Coach Michael Burt, Bridges with Monica Schmelter, TCT's Nashville Today, Bloom Today, Power Fueled Living, and Ring of Faith. Christy lives in Tennessee with her husband, daughter, and three bonus children.

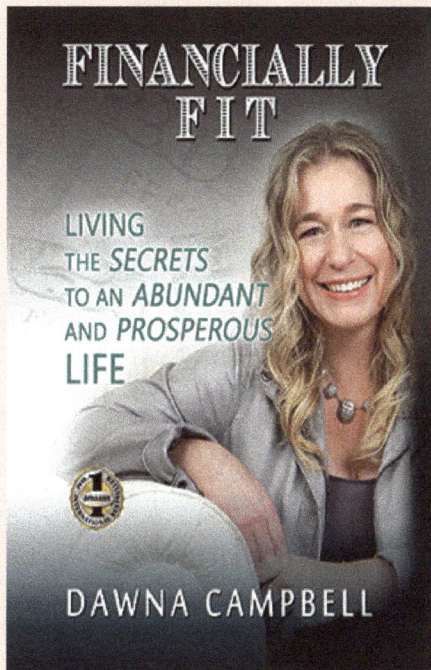

Financial Coach and Author Dawna Campbell: Living the Secrets to an Abundant and Prosperous Life

Being financially fit is about having a mindset and heart-set that is open to money and abundance." — Dawna Campbell

BIGFORK, MT, USA, February 25, 2021 /EINPresswire.com/ -- "When the words 'financially fit' are heard, there is an initial impression of how to invest, eliminate debt, and create a world of wealth" says financial lifestyle author Dawna Campbell. "If this is your initial impression, then I might disappoint you."

Over the last 25 years of her professional career, Campbell discovered a problem; the disconnect between the energy of money and what is in the deep subconscious.

"When outdated patterns and programs are released, aligned, and transformed with the energy of money, instant abundance and prosperity are the result. "Financially Fit" is the perfect financial book for the person who wants to be fit in their mind financially first, then utilize all the money tools and rules given by financial gurus," she said.

As a former Financial Advisor and Managing Principal, Campbell believed that she knew about money, but after hospital time, and a divorce, she found herself filing for bankruptcy as a single parent. She had followed the rules that we're taught about money, health, and relationships, yet her abundance stream was cut off. She soon discovered that being financially fit is about more than budgets, savings, mutual funds, bonds, insurance, and real estate.

"Being financially fit is about having a mindset and heartset that is open to money and abundance," she said. Campbell empowers heart-centered business owners to realign their inner balance to gain infinite prosperity.

"Many people strive to be financially fit, but few people understand the energy that surrounds money and how thoughts can increase or decrease the personal money supply," she said. Campbell teaches readers how powerful our thoughts are.

By changing how the feelings behind the thoughts with money, the abundance flow can magnetically attract back creating unlimited wealth. Some of the lessons in Dawna Campbell's book, "Financially Fit: Living the Secrets to an Abundant and Prosperous Life" include:
• How to implement the three secret keys to bring in prosperity.
• How to avoid money and energy debts.
• How to release self-sabotaging money-inhibiting patterns.
• How to rebuild your money surplus and energy supply.
• How to create your financial affluence story.

International Author William O. Joseph, says "In these troubled times it is fitting that her new book, "Financially Fit," reveals how to acquire an inner state of abundance in our common quest to manifest prosperity in every aspect of our lives."

With thought and feelings being so powerful, we have the power to change the way that money appears in our personal life. Financially Fit does just that, bridging the gap between the financial world, with the heart, mind, and soul of the energy body.

About Dawna Campbell

Known as the Mind Whisperer, Dawna Campbell combines her past knowledge, wisdom, and experience to assist you in creating and restoring a life of happiness, prosperity, and love. Dawna has over 25 years combined years of professional experience.

As a former Financial Advisor, her book, "Financially Fit," is a #1 Amazon International Best Seller which brings together the world of money and the energy body, and the soul's essence.

She is a professional speaker and maintains an international private practice. Dawna has shared the stage with Lisa Nichols, Dr. Joe Vitale, Sharon Lechter, and David Meltzer. Her personal Heart Centered Healing philosophy is to create a world that is a better place.

For more information: https://dawnacampbell.com

5 TIPS

Children Benefit

5 Ways Children Benefit From Creative Playtime

Movement helps children hone their coordination, balance and motor skills. Associating exercise with fun can set a precedent for a lifetime habit.

When kids pretend to be their favorite superhero, it may look like sheer fun at first glance, but experts say that imaginative play also benefits children in a number of substantial ways.

"From building confidence and self-perception to offering children an opportunity to practice communication and language skills, pretend play is vital to child development," says Keri Wilmot, a pediatric occupational therapist and an expert contributor to TheGeniusofPlay.org.

How can creative play help your child thrive? Here are five important benefits, according to The Genius of Play, a national movement providing families with the information, inspiration and hands-on ideas they need to make play an important part of their child's day.

• **Enhanced literacy:** Some of the same mental connections that take place when a child is first learning to read are employed in the world of pretend. Whether it's a banana that becomes a phone or a towel being used as a cape, grasping symbolism in the world of play can pave the way for children to better recognize that each letter of the alphabet represents a sound. Encourage kids to use the everyday objects and toys around them to build a world of creativity and fun.

• **Leadership skills:** From a very young age, playtime experiences can

IMAGE: PEXELS

have a major impact on the development of children's leadership skills. In the case of superhero play, the act of taking on a powerful persona offers kids an opportunity to assert themselves and gain self-confidence, while creatively constructing their own story lines. Through play, parents, teachers and mentors can help foster these attributes in children.

• **Movement:** Movement helps children hone their coordination, balance and motor skills. Associating exercise with fun can set a precedent for a lifetime habit. What's more, physical activity encourages better eating and sleeping habits. Be sure your kids have a safe place to play indoors that lets them burn off all their energy. When the weather is nice, take the fun to the backyard or a nearby park, where the possibilities for pretend expand.

• **Perseverance:** Known as the "Batman Effect," a 2016 study published in "Child Development" found that kids stay better focused on a task when they are pretending to be their favorite superheroes or characters. Through play, you can encourage your children to channel the bravery and perseverance of the superheroes they admire most, giving them the emotional tools needed to thrive in a challenging world.

• **Emotional development:** Role play offers children an opportunity to explore their emotions, both good and bad, while building compassion. Children can channel frustration, anger, fear and triumph into the worlds, characters and storylines they create, learning to manage these emotions in healthy ways. For more child development tips and play resources, visit TheGeniusofPlay.org.

There may be times when you'd prefer your child finally change out of his or her superhero costume. But by letting kids explore their creativity, you can help them reap the benefits of this type of play.

ONE LONDON DAY

A New Direction In Crime By International Bestselling Author and Arthur Ellis Award Winner Chris (CC) Humphreys

"Chris Humphreys imbues this tale with the art of weaving, not only as the core of this book, but also in the manner in which he so deftly positions reality with fantasy – a true and splendid tapestry of a story that primes for the next installments in this Tapestry Trilogy. Very highly recommended!"
 - Grady Harp, Top 100 Reviewer for Amazon and Top Shelf Magazine

It's the hottest Summer in fifty years and Joseph Severin, a respectable North London businessman, has taken on a lucrative side job. He's doing the books, old school, (because these days the only trail you can't trace is a paper one) for a rogue MI5 outfit, the Shadows, headed by clever, psychopathic Sebastien. When the game is rumbled, he sends their hitman, Mr Phipps, to kill Severin and get those books back.

For a simple man, Severin has a complicated life. He's developed a sudden and wild passion for Lottie – aka 'chaos on two legs'. Who is in love with Patrick, the next hot young black actor. Who is obsessed by Sonya, a gorgeous Russian escort. Who has one night to make the final money she needs for her daughter's cancer operation. With MI6 onto them, and the books missing, the Shadows panic. And a day that begins with a hit in Finchley ends in violence and betrayal on the steamy night streets of Portobello.

ONE LONDON DAY is a daisy chain tale of characters and connections, a contemporary London Noir. Like that genre's 40's origins, this story has its hood, its moll, its femme fatale, its fancy boy. Everyone is both protagonist and antagonist. No one gets out unharmed – and some don't get out at all.

CC HUMPHREYS

ONE LONDON DAY

Wilma Adelmund-Conrads' New Book

'Florence' is an Enthralling Novel That Focuses on the Story of Friendship, Family, and Courage

"Florence" from Newman Springs Publishing author Wilma Adelmund-Conrads is a thrilling narrative that follows the journey of a woman who has experienced a devastation in her life and became a victim of undeviating fear.

Wilma Adelmund-Conrads, a dynamic author who loves reading and writing, has completed her new book "Florence": a captivating tome that will leave the readers in awe as the author reveals a thrilling journey of a woman who never thought of giving up because of the hope that she sees in her family and friends.

Wilma writes, "Set in a small town in Iowa during WWII, a beautiful young woman experiences her own type of war. As a victim of constant fear, she finds refuge in her friendship with a kind, hardworking couple who intervenes.

"As in any war, there must be some sort of victory which many times comes through the kindness of true friends who assist in fighting a common enemy. Through many a conflict, true friends and family are the keys to a difficult but hopeful conclusion, regardless of its outcome."

Florence

Wilma Adelmund-Conrads

Published by Newman Springs Publishing, Conrads' gripping
tale allows readers to realize that they can always find hope
and courage in their family and friends whenever they are
experiencing the darkest hours of their lives.

In this book, the readers will come to see and relate themselves
to how the main character thrives to survive the war she has
experienced as she walks through her journey.

7 Reasons Why Poetry Is Good for the Soul

Poetry is a great therapy, which helps you understand and convey your feelings and thoughts. Typically, poetry is brief but involve

By Shalini M

This is the era of Digital Age, which means most of youngsters and adults prefer the 140-character model of communication. Many of us use Facebook to share what we love. This has diverted our attention from the importance of poetry, which was a common medium of expression a few decades back. Poetry introduces us to the magic of simplicity, complexity, the use of our senses, and the metaphor, to name a few. Let's us why poetry is good for your inner piece.

1. Developmental Learning

The conventional education system of today curbs the written and verbal skills of children. But poetry can help them how to put different words together to create a rhythm and develop their cognitive understanding of tons of words. Moreover, it helps kids understand the art of expression through words.

2. Developing Skills

Poetry has a great impact on your speaking, writing and understanding. Rules are meant to be followed, but poetry teaches you how you can break these rules and still maintain beauty in a piece of writing.
So, poetry is a great way of developing your skills so you can get the most out of your skills.

3. THERAPY For The Readers

Poetry is also a great therapy, which helps you understand and convey your feelings and thoughts. Typically, poetry is brief but involves sentiments. Today, anxiety and depression are two most common psychological problems that the Biblio-therapy can treat.

4. Therapeutic For The Readers

If you find it hard to express yourself, you can read poetry to improve your way of expression. If you read poetry, you can get a deeper insight into the mindset of another person. So, poetry has therapeutic effect on the reader as well.

5. The Significance Of Words

As far as the design is concerned, poetry can be divided into short but powerful sentences. If you read poetry, you can understand the importance of a variety of words and the way they can be used to construct effective sentences. At times, the placement of words changes the meaning or rhythm of the entire poem.

6. Understanding People

Today, people find it hard to understand each other. Frustration is the result of misunderstanding or miscommunication. On the other hand, poetry can help people hone their ability to understand others.
You can get deeper into the parts of your statement that they find hard to understand. You also learn to be more patient and tolerate others while they are saying things against you.

7. Understanding Yourself

You may have found yourself in a situation where no one seems to understand you. We all haven here at some point in our lives. Writing poetry is one way of grasping your internal turmoil. It helps you convert your thoughts into comprehensive thoughts.
So, these are some of the most compelling reasons why you may want to start reading and writing poetry today. Hope this will help you use poetry to achieve your inner peace and lead a better life in addition to help others.

Source: EzineArticles

FOR WOMEN: DAILY MOTIVATION
How to Be More Active in Your Daily Life

Are you struggling to get out of bed now that there is lockdown almost everywhere in the world? There is a bright side to the current situation. Motivate yourself to push yourself through the day to be more active and enjoy life indoors. This article shows how. Here is a set of pointers to get you through the day:

BY ROSINA S KHAN

1. First thing in the morning, make your bed.

2. Next wash up and meditate or pray. Pray for your family, city, country and the world.

3. Recite holy verses from the Holy Book relevant to the current situation so that you feel peace at heart.

4. Then look over your email box. Answer one or two or just go through. Keep an email account just to receive positive and upbeat self-help content.

5. Go over social media content. Like whatever eye-catching posts you come across and post your own ideas so that others are attracted to your post.

6. Have breakfast. Bread and jam and a glass of orange juice are quite good to have. But you can have your own preferred choices.

7. Then make time for reading. I like reading Sidney Sheldon novels and self-help eBooks, which keep me preoccupied for two hours or more.

8. Then do a bit of cleaning around. Sweep the floors and mop accordingly making your surroundings immaculate.

9. Water your plants in tubs or garden and enjoy a bit of the sunshine.

10. Carry out your laundry.

11. Wipe out the surfaces of tables, chairs, dressing table, sink, cabinets, washing machine and any surface you can find. Get rid of all the germs this way.

12. If you have children and a hubby, share with them, eating breakfast.

13. Ask your hubby to play with your children for some time while you start cooking for them.

14. Share delicious yummy homemade lunch with family.

15. Ask your hubby to finish cleaning the table and the dishes while you put down the children for an afternoon nap.

16. You and your hubby can watch an adult movie while your children sleep.

17. Start preparing late afternoon snacks such as French toast, cereal, potato chips etc. that your children would like after they wake up.

18. Read out to them children's story books and play making handicrafts out of paper and clay.

19. Sit with their school lessons and do some homeschooling.

20. Let them draw and color on sheets of paper and get them busy while you and your hubby work from home.

21. Prepare dinner with a helping hand from your hubby and sit together and enjoy the dishes. Clean the dishes and ask your hubby to read bedtime stories to your children, gradually letting them fall asleep.

22. So it was a productive day in your own way, staying indoors. Keep some time for self-care before you retire to bed.

Summing up, the above pointers show how you can motivate yourself to be more active and productive throughout the day, instead of lying in bed idly, not taking any responsibility. You must also be an example to your family, your neighborhood and the community so that unitedly we can overcome the deadly situation of current times.

Rosina S Khan has authored this article. For a wealth of free resources based on stunning fiction stories and academic guides, amazing self-help eBooks, articles and blogs, all authored by her, and much more, visit: https://rosinaskhan.weebly.com. You will be glad that you did.

Source: EzineArticles

Advice

FASHION

Fashions are constantly
changing
&
so look for some
basic items of clothing
that you can add to
&
create a new look. A
great fitting pair of black
pants are the basic look
you can dress up or dress
down
&
as well as wear in sum-
mer or during the winter
months.

Are you a fashion aficio-
nado who stands proudly?
Or is it that you are not
fashionably inclined? Either
way, you can appreciate
some up to date fashion
advice. This article provides
some valuable fashion tips
that anyone can use.

Advice

Fashion Advice
That Everyone Could Use

Dress in a way that accurately reflects your age. If you are a young professional woman, do not go to work dressed like someone in their teens. On the other hand, if you are a teenager, do not dress in a style that an older woman would feel comfortable in. Don't be afraid to top off your look with an awesome hat. In days gone by, it was commonplace for women and men to wear hats on a daily basis. What was once the height of fashion has, unfortunately, fallen to the wayside in modern times. Be adventurous, and finish off your look with an ultra-cool fedora or a pretty sun hat. To sweep hair from your shoulders, try a casual updo. When you're having a busy work day or school day, long hair is a pain. When there's no time to mess with your hair, simply use an elastic to sweep your locks into a messy-but-charming bun.If you like form fitting clothing, it is very important to know what materials and colors blend together, and will hold their form the best. This is significant because if you get the wrong blend not only the outfit will possibly go out of shape, but it might

be uncomfortable as well. A very important fashion tip is to make sure that your pants are the correct length. This is important because having pants that are too long or short can be a critical mistake in looking good. Be sure to plan for the type of shoes that you will be wearing because it will make a huge difference. If you are going to go somewhere in the world of fashion, you need to understand that fashion is not all about the right outfits. Your makeup is just as important as the clothes that you wear. Finding the right makeup style and accessorizing properly can bring your fashion to a whole new world. During the summer, you should avoid wearing excess makeup. In the summer, it can get very hot. Therefore, it is not good to wear heavy makeups. A lighter makeup style for the summer will ideally complement your fun summer style, keeping your skin healthy, and you will looking perfectly fashionable.

EXPERIENTIALITY travel design boutique

aims to restore normalcy in vacations

back to pre-pandemic normal

In angst-ridden times, Experientiality has your back with a plan so airtight not even a micro virus can disrupt it

HOUSTON, TEXAS, UNITED STATES,
March 26, 2021

xperientialty, (www.Experientiality.com), the experiential travel design boutique of renown, aims to restore life back to the dearly missed pre-pandemic normal.

Ask yourself this: What exactly are you going to do if you catch the Covid-19 virus? With whom is your first call? How are you going to make sure you have the best available care ?

Amid this Covid-19 landscape, Experientiality is making travel more manageable by creating increased comfort levels while alleviating the hassles associated with Covid-19 regulations.

Experientiality's Prevention, Extraction or Retreat offers a pandemic-safe vacation plan executed on the ground by expert staff within a command center, always at-the-ready to tackle unforeseen circumstances.

Gregory Patrick (a.k.a The DreamMaker) has crafted a comprehensive threefold program:

Stage I begins by mitigating the virus at home. Sanitation and hygiene protocols are strictly implemented with the company's hand picked staff to ensure a sterile environment. Your resident PhD. (infectologist) spends the day-time sanitizing all grocery and restaurant deliveries with high-intensity UV lights, virucides and other virus protection measures.

Diminishing contagion and touch points is mission critical.

Stage II, "retreat" is hardly such, even at the most stunning resorts, when one is forced to wear masks while wandering the grounds, dining, swimming and, holy smoke, even at the beach! Suddenly, "high-tech" replaces "high-touch" and the human experience that has us plop down $1,500 a night.

Experientiality has your back with its "Hotel-at-Home" experience. All staff are quarantined for two weeks prior to your arrival and a geofence (virtual

boundary) monitors all staff movements 24/7. Experientiality has devised a rather clever solution for yacht charters as well.

Your Hotel-at-Home staff are at-your-service when trans-

as medical evacuation may not be possible without it.

With Experientiliaty's contracted experts, the affected will be transported to a private hospital suite supplied with the needed medical equipment. Moreover, a top-ranked pulmonary physician and two carefully chosen nurses will cover two shifts, constantly monitoring the patient's recovery.

"Advance planning proves to be the lifesaver that makes all the difference," says Mr. Patrick. If something happens, there must be a predetermined plan executed with military precision and there's no time to waste going back and forth with call centers (as to eligible coverage).

ferring to your Supercoach for unique excursions.

"Your country estate is in geographical proximity to hospitals nationally ranked in their pulmonary subspecialty. We're loaded for bear if you need to receive medical attention," says Mr. Patrick.

Stage III >>> BREAK GLASS - GMTFO, A family member suffering a stroke (or life threatening complications) is just as affected if all the beds are locked up. An airtight medical solution must be fully tailored. Upon receipt of a non-refundable $30,000 retainer, Experientiality will organize a full medical in-home work-up by a respected M.D.

Advance planning proves to be the lifesaver that makes all the difference"
— Mr. Gregory Patrick

Is There Enough Creativity in Your Life?

"The scientific community knows that creativity offers huge benefits to individuals, both directly and via benefits to health and happiness," says Mark Runco, director of Creativity Research and Programming at Southern Oregon University.

New research suggests that Americans may be picking up paint brushes over remote controls.

Two-thirds of adults in a recent survey say they seek to use their creativity more in life, and 77 percent would rather give up their Netflix subscription for a year than their favorite creative hobby. The study, conducted by Bluprint, NBCUniversal's state-of-the-art digital lifestyle learning platform and streaming service, in partnership with IPSOS, explores the growth of creativity, and what brings people joy in 2019.

"What's clear is that Americans crave a greater sense of personal fulfillment," says Catherine Balsam-Schwaber, GM of Bluprint. "This may be the first time in American history that mothers are wishing for their children to be starving artists rather than wealthy and unhappy." This is good news, as experts say that creativity has the potential to make people happier and improve their overall well-being.

"The scientific community knows that creativity offers huge benefits to individuals, both directly and via benefits to health and happiness," says Mark Runco, director of Creativity Research and Programming at Southern Oregon University.

The survey also revealed the following insights:

• Doctor prescribed creativity: Science has legitimized creativity as a critical component of well-being, and doctors are increasingly prescribing creative pursuits as part of medical prescription regimens. If given the choice, 57 percent of U.S. adults would rather take up a new creative hobby than start a new medication, if assured by their doctor it would have the same health benefits.

• Handmade happiness: The majority of those surveyed love both the process of making something from scratch, as well as the joy they received from the finished project. Three in four U.S. adults currently participate in at least one creative activity, with baking, gardening, cooking (beyond everyday meals), home décor and DIY crafting being the most popular.

• Happy accidents: Success as an end-goal is increasingly being put on the back-burner, as more people realize that mistakes are just a natural part of the creative journey. Indeed, 75 percent of those surveyed say making a mistake doesn't take away from their enjoyment in what they're creating.

• Parents on board: Seventy-seven percent of parents want their children to have more opportunities to be creative than they did when they were young. In thinking about their future, 79 percent would rather their children make just enough to get by in a creative job that they love, over making lots of money in a job they aren't passionate about. Unfortunately, in parents' eyes, today's education system doesn't place enough emphasis on creativity, with 61 percent agreeing that public education lacks creative arts focus and 72 percent saying that standardized test scores are prioritized more than creative thinking.

• Ego Booster: Participation in creative activities also appears to have a positive influence on adults' perceptions of themselves. Those who participate in creative activities are more likely than those who don't to describe themselves as optimistic, happy, passionate and joyful.

To learn more about Bluprint, offering thousands of hours of content in categories such as crafting, knitting, wellness, cooking, baking, fitness and more, as well as access to curated supplies and a supportive community, visit mybluprint.com.

When focusing on your health, happiness and well-being, don't forget the importance of finding outlets that allow you to explore your everyday creativity.

(StatePoint)

Shero Comics Celebrates
Black History Month with the Return of the Rayven Choi Graphic Novel Series

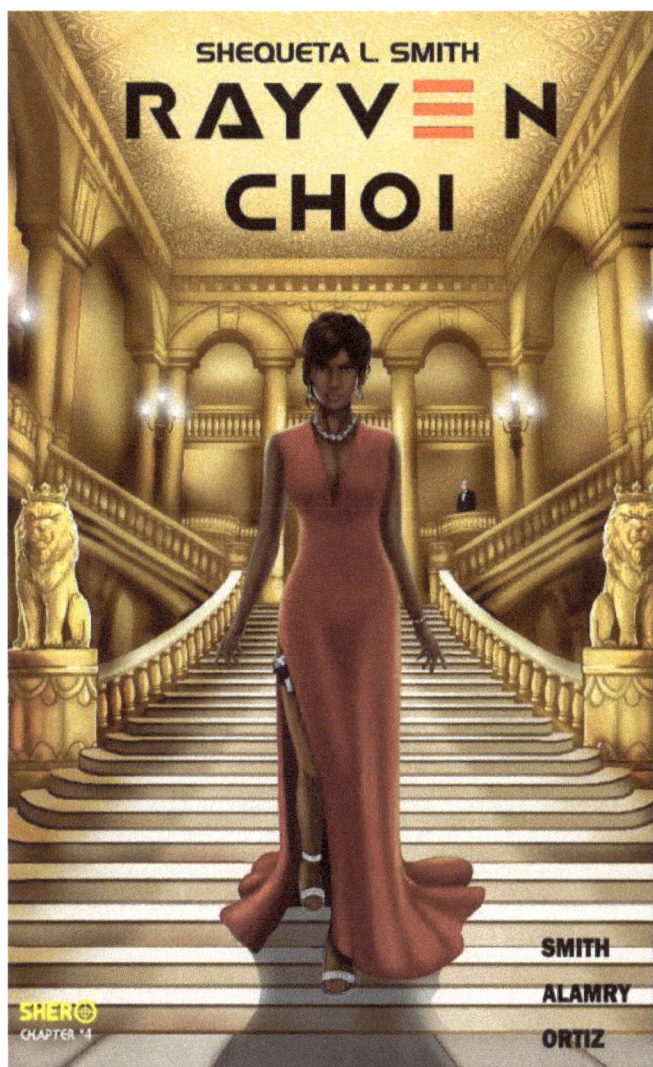

After a successful world tour, the release of three books, launching an all-female comic con, and a short stint writing a feature film in Ron Howard and Brian Grazer's screenwriting incubator, Imagine Impact 2, comic book creator Shequeta Smith returns this week with the release of the fourth book in her award-winning five-part graphic novel series, "Rayven Choi."

Rayven Choi is a gripping, coming-of-age story about an African American girl who is orphaned and sent to South Korea to preserve her safety. Rayven uncovers a shocking secret in the prequels and vows to avenge the death of her parents. In the upcoming fourth chapter, Rayven Choi: Chasing Ghosts, Rayven comes face to face with the hitman who murdered her parents all those years ago and gets one step closer to getting the revenge that she seeks.

Smith, a North Carolina native who in between creating comics, moonlights as a Hollywood screenwriter, is excited to continue the series.

"After traveling the international comic-con circuit with the Shero Universe tour, and stopping to write for Hollywood, it's been a long journey to get back to Rayven Choi, but I couldn't be more excited. Being able to release this book during Black History Month feels like a superpower," said Smith.

Smith's Shero Universe tour featured stops at comic conventions in Seoul, South Korea; Jakarta, Indonesia; Pyeongtaek, South Korea; Los Angeles and New York City. During the tour, cameras followed Smith as she successfully introduced her Rayven Choi series to new fans across the globe. Shero Comics is expected to release the globetrotting docuseries, "The Shero Universe" later this year.

Rayven Choi: Chasing Ghosts is now accepting pre-orders on Amazon Kindle and is scheduled to be released this Friday, February 19, 2021. Digital copies of the previous books in the Rayven Choi series are now available on Amazon Kindle and ComiXology. Physical copies of the books, as well as accompanying merchandise, are available in the Shero Comics webstore.

RockBrash Promotions Announces

German Edition Release Of Rahaman Ali's New Book My Brother Muhammad Ali

ATLANTA - Feb. 19, 2021 - Rahaman Ali, the younger brother of the late Muhammad Ali, who is managed and promoted by ROCKBRASH PROMOTIONS, has his new book, MEIN BRUDER, MUHAMMAD ALI which is the German translation of MY BROTHER, MUHAMMAD ALI – THE DEFINITIVE BIOGRAPHY By Rahaman Ali with Fiaz Rafiq and foreword by NFL Legend Jim Brown, along with an endorsement by former Heavyweight Champion of the World, Mike Tyson, was released in Germany on February 15, 2021.

Originally published (British English) by London-based John Blake Publishing, an imprint of Bonnier Books UK on October 17, 2019.

After a very successful launch in the United Kingdom which yielded rave reviews from practically all of the Top British National Papers, and the book winning a prestigious SUNDAY TIMES BOOK OF THE YEAR AWARD, My Brother, Muhammad Ali – The Definitive Biography made its USA release debut on Friday, October 09, 2020! The USA edition (American English) is published by Rowman & Littlefield. Then on October 20th, 2020, the French Edition of the book titled MOHAMED ALI, MON FRERE which is published by Editions Alisio was released in France. Then the Hungarian Edition of the book titled TESTVEREM, MUHAMMAD ALI which is published by Cartaphilus Publishing in Hungary was released on November 20th, 2020, followed by Russian Edition of the book titled мой брат мохаммед али which is published by AST Publishing in Russia.

Now comes the German Edition of the book titled MEIN BRUDER, MUHAMMAD ALI which is published by Egoth Publishing, and is headquartered in Vienna, Austria.

When asked what it means to have his new book released in the UK, the USA, translated in the French language and released in France, translated in the Hungarian language and released in Hungary, translated in Russian and released in Russia, and now translated in the German language Rahaman stated, "I am overwhelmed with joy by witnessing the global support that my book is receiving."

RockBrash Promotions CEO - Ron Brashear followed with, "Its an honor to have Mr Ali's book now translated in the German language. Moreover, we look forward to working closely with Egoth Verlag publishing to further promote this most historically significant book every written on Muhammad Ali by the man who knew him best - his own brother."

The CEO of Egoth Publishing stated, "Let me underline the fact how proud we are to have this book in our program. It is a very special Ali biography and cannot be compared to the tons of others which already exist." - Egon Theiner

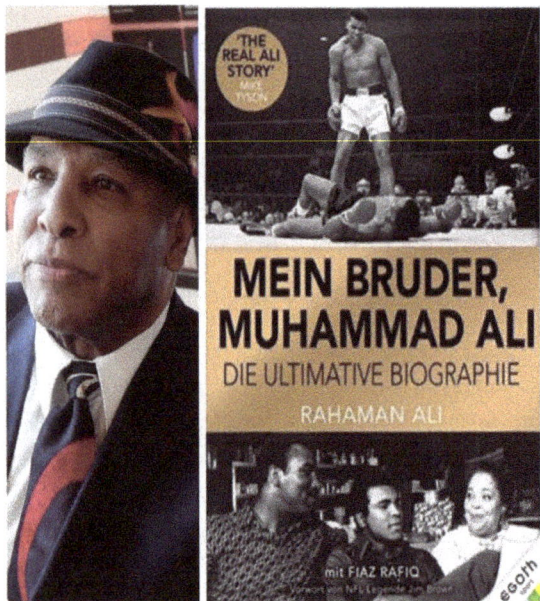

Titled Mein Bruder, Muhammad Ali which is the German translation of the book My Brother, Muhammad Ali

Sammie Strange's New Book

'A Strange Life' Accounts an Awe-Inspiring Journey Across the Struggles of Poverty During the Great Depression

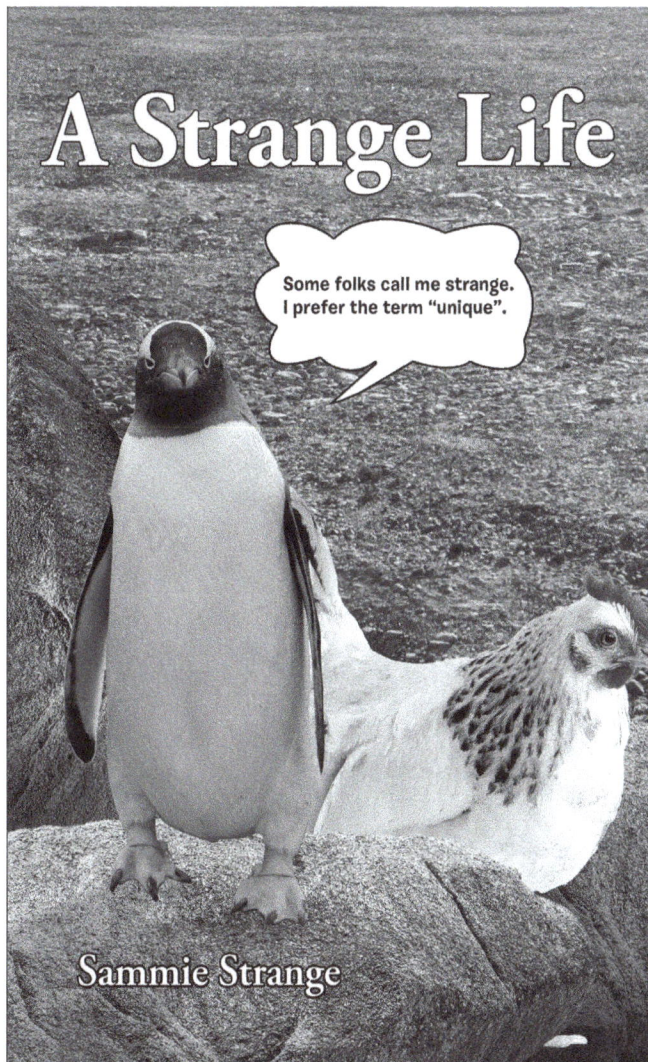

A Strange Life

Some folks call me strange. I prefer the term "unique".

Sammie Strange

TEXARKANA, Texas, March 4, 2021 (Newswire.com) - Sammie Strange, a brilliant author, has completed his new book "A Strange Life": a profound narrative that speaks of will, bravery, and unity in a journey that was plagued with challenges yet has found a way to stand against the world and stand tall at life.

Sammie writes, "A book about a boy and his family and how they struggled through The Great Depression, a father's early death that left a mother with six children and only farming and family skills, in bad health with no insurance or means to earn a living, no home, no car, and seven dollars to pay on a grave site. This is a story of that boy's life."

Published by Newman Springs Publishing, Sammie Strange's inspirational memoir will bring much encouragement and hope from a life that was able to overcome the hurdles of the 1900s.

This is a testament of a life worth telling.

Readers who wish to experience this excellent work can purchase "A Strange Life" at bookstores everywhere, or online at the Apple iBooks Store, Amazon, or Barnes and Noble.

www.ingramcontent.com/pod-product-compliance
Lightning Source LLC
Chambersburg PA
CBHW052348210326
41597CB00037B/6297